Uplift

A Little Book
of God's Promises to Give Hope
and Uplift Your Soul

By Natalia Terfa

WISE
CREATIVE + PUBLISHING
Ink
2012

ISBN: 978-1-945769-23-8
eISBN: 978-1-945769-24-5
Library of Congress Catalog Number: 2016956687

Printed in the United States of America
First Printing: 2016
20   19 18   17   16   5   4   3   2   1

Cover Design by Emily Rodvold

Wise Ink Creative Publishing
837 Glenwood Ave.
Minneapolis, MN 55405
www.wiseinkpub.com

*To Sue, who asked me to start writing these
in the first place, and who teaches me about grace and
faith and trust with each and every conversation.*

Contents

Introduction

NOT TOO LONG INTO my first year of pastoral ministry at Prince of Peace, I was asked to help create a cancer support group. At that time, it felt like everyone had cancer—all these amazing people were struggling, and there was a need for a place to pray and encourage each other. So POP-HOPE (Prince of Peace Helping Each Other in Prayer and Encouragement) was born. This little group has been faithfully meeting monthly for three years, and it is amazing. So amazing. Each time we gather, prayers are said, tears are shed (we often joke about the Kleenex box making the rounds with our check-ins), and so much love and support is extended.

In the fall of our second year of meeting, a member of the group asked if I'd be willing to write a devotion once a week to help offer hope and a little extra lift. I figured it was a small thing I could do to help those in this exclusive club. So that first week, I sat down at my desk to write, and the Friday Uplift was born.

Since then, almost one hundred emails later, Uplift has grown from a small, twelve-person email list to a movement. The devotions were shared, people asked to be added to the list, more were shared, and it just kept on growing.

And growing.

And I learned that everyone needs an uplift.

Seriously.

Everyone.

Our world often seems like the opposite of uplifting. People can be mean and quick to judge and point out flaws, and the world around us is often discouraging and disappointing. Somehow my little group of e-mail recipients found a hole that needed to be filled with positivity. So with every Uplift that was forwarded, printed out, and mailed, the Uplift community soon transformed from Upliftees to Uplifters.

Each share and forward got to a person who needed it. And that reader learned what we had all learned in this Uplift movement—we are not alone. We're a community.

There isn't a person alive who hasn't had a day or week or month or even year where they needed an extra bit of hope or encouragement.

That's why this book came to be.

Because we've all been there.

Maybe you're there now, or maybe you know someone who is there now.

Life isn't easy.

At all.

And it is in the darkest, most difficult times where we need a lift.

A moment of hope.

Like a flower blooming through concrete.

Or a single balloon rising up in the sky,

We all need it.
All of us.

So that's what this is.
A little bit of hope in a little bitty book.
Let it lift you.
And then, pass it on.
Join the movement.
Be an uplifter.

Hope

May the God of hope fill you with
all joy and peace in believing,
so that you may abound in hope by the
power of the Holy Spirit.

ROMANS 15:13

HOPE. EASY TO SAY, HARDER TO DO.

I always have wondered how we get hope. If I'm feeling a hopeless, how do I go about becoming more hopeful?

Believe it or not, the word *hope* is not often used in the New Testament—it only appears fifty-four times—and never appears in the Gospels. (It only appears thirty-two times in the Hebrew equivalent in the Old Testament.)

In the New Testament the word *elpis* (pronounced el-peace), is often translated as hope. Elpis literally means "an expectation of something good."

Read that again.

An expectation of something good.

Not just maybe, perhaps something good . . .
but expecting something good.

I think we use hope like it's not a given.

We say, "I hope so!"

and "My fingers are crossed" and "I'm hoping for the best!"

But that's not what the word means.

Hope is an expectation that good is going to happen.

Not potential for good, but expectation of good.

At the root of hopelessness is the fear or belief that good
things cannot and will not happen to us.

Sometimes we really feel this way.

We cry out to God:

Stop!

Please don't let me take one more hit!

I can't take another piece of bad news!

And as we wonder how on earth we are supposed to
manage,

we start to believe that maybe good things really won't come
to us.

And I get it—I've been there—but let me say this loudly and clearly today:

that is not truth.

God has promised to give us good things.

In Matthew 7, Jesus is talking to his followers about this very thing:

"Ask, and it will be given you; search, and you will find; knock, and the door will be opened for you . . . Is there anyone among you who, if your child asks for bread, will give a stone? Or if the child asks for a fish, will give a snake? If you then, who are evil, know how to give good gifts to your children, how much more will your Father in heaven give good things to those who ask him!

For those who have kids, it's hard to imagine responding to their request for something to eat with a rock. And—and this is important—we are *not* God.

So if it is possible for us non-God people to give good things to our children, imagine the good things God is going to give *you.*

This is where hope comes from.

From God, who has promised to give us good things.

Hear that today.

Believe that you are God's beloved child.

Trust that God will keep his promises, and expect good things.

That is hope.

not Alone

Moses' father-in-law replied, 'What you
are doing is not good. You and those
people who come to you will only wear
yourselves out. The work is too heavy
for you; you cannot handle it alone.'

EXODUS 18:17–18

OKAY, I ADMIT THAT at first glance these two verses may
not seem all that uplifting—but I promise, they really are.
Really. Because Jethro, Moses' father-in-law, is speaking the
truth here, and that truth is a message we all need to hear.

Stop trying to do it on your own.

Do you need me to say it again?

Stop trying to do it on your own.

Moses is trying to help everyone.

He is trying to do it all.

He isn't a bad guy; he has great intentions. He doesn't want to burden anyone else, so he just tries to take care of things on his own.

And it's killing him and frustrating those around him.

Moses' father-in-law comes for a visit and offers some advice to his exhausted son: Stop, Moses. Just stop.

I love it.

Jethro doesn't sugarcoat things at all here.

He doesn't say, "I see what you're trying to do here Moses, and that's really noble of you." Nope.

He bluntly says that what's happening is not good for anyone and it needs to stop.

We've all been there.

We've all been Moses.

Trying to do it all.

Trying to be everything to everyone.

Trying to make sure everyone is happy.

Trying to take care of others when we need someone to take care of us.

And now Jethro and I are here to tell you to stop.

Just stop.

This is where the uplift comes in.

Because when you ask for help, when you invite others into your life to share in your burden, you become lighter.

I promise.

That's the gift, the pure gift, of being a part of a community of faith: we never, ever, have to do life alone. Never.

This means that when we are good, when our faith is strong and our experience of grace is overflowing, there is always someone next to us who needs our support. Who needs to be held up. So hold them up.

And if the person in need of help is you—then stop doing it on your own and ask for help.

We are created to be in community.

So stop doing it alone.

Stop holding it in.

Stop bearing your grief, your illness, your struggles, the weights in your life, all by yourself.

It is not good.

I repeat: it is not good.

So today, if you are feeling weak—if you are the Moses in this story—my prayer is that you say yes.

Say yes when someone asks if there is anything they can do.

Say yes when someone asks if they can pray for you.

Say yes when someone asks if they can bring you a meal.

Say yes when someone asks if you need to talk.

Say yes if you need a hug.

Say yes if you need to be distracted.

Just say yes.

As Jethro reminds Moses, "That will make your load lighter, because they will share it with you."

In his second letter to the Corinthians, Paul says, "Your abundance may be a supply for their need."

If you are feeling good today, if you are feeling strong and loved in abundance, then be Jethro for someone else. Help someone carry their burden today.

Offer to make them a meal,

sit and be with them,

bring over ice cream and movies,

drive them to an appointment,

pray for them and with them, or do whatever they need.

Remind someone that they are not alone, that they never ever have to do life alone.

Because it's true.

God promised we'll never be alone.

And then God gave us himself, and then gave us to each other, and told us to get to it.

So let's get to it.

Light

The people who walked in darkness
have seen a great light;
those who lived in a land of deep
darkness—on them light has shined.

ISAIAH 9:2

I KNOW THERE ARE a lot of people out there who will disagree with me, but I'm just going to say it:

I'd take a really cold and sunny day over a warm and cloudy one every time.

In the frozen north of Minnesota—where I live—we have a lot of bitterly cold sunny days.

But we have a lot of cloudy and not-so-cold ones, too.

And those are the days that just get to me.

It saps all of my energy to not see the sun shining; I just *long* for the clouds to clear.

So this verse is a good reminder for me.

Because not being able to see the sun doesn't mean it's not there.

And a few clouds today don't mean it won't be sunny tomorrow.

There are going to be some days that are overcast.

In fact, some days are going to be downright dark.

But it is on those days I can remember the sun.

I have seen a great light.

I can remember that.

Light shines on me in my darkest moments.

I can remember this too.

God has promised to be with us, to send us light.

And darkness cannot overcome the light.

Neither can a cloudy day.

And that longing for the sun? That's good too.

It keeps us open, awake, and alert.

It keeps our eyes open for those moments of the light breaking into the dark.

For the light to overtake the gloom.

For the weather to change and the clouds to float away.

No matter what, we can trust that the light is always there.

Always shining.

In my family, on cloudy summer days, we always say, "It'll burn off."

It's a long-standing joke.

We usually say this when we're at the lake or have outdoor plans, when we're hoping that the day can be salvaged.

We are always holding out hope that the sun will work hard and break through the clouds.

So when life seems a little overcast and the light is hard to see—remember that light will again break through the darkness.

Even the smallest bit of light can do a lot in a dark place. The darkness has never won and will never win.

Even when it feels like you are in your darkest day, I promise—and better yet, God promises—it'll burn off.

Freedom

For freedom Christ has set us free.
Stand firm, therefore, and do not submit
again to a yoke of slavery.

GALATIANS 5:1

WE HAVE BEEN SET free by Christ, Paul writes to us in his letter to Galatians.

It's more than just a nice turn of phrase—it is an important reminder.

You are set free.

Free from illness.

Free from depression.

Free from fear.

Free from whatever it is that is enslaving you.

You have been set free.

Christ is constantly coming into our lives and breaking the chains which entrap us.

But sometimes we don't see this.

We get stuck in our fear, in our sadness, in our shame,

and we willingly let those chains continue to bind us.

This is what Paul warns against.

"Stand firm," he writes.

He uses the Greek word *steko*, which means "to stand against, to persevere."

Do not submit again to the life you had before Christ. Stand firm, persevere.

You are free!

My stepdad sent me this picture, and I think it fits so well with this verse.

It is a picture about changing perspective, but it's also a reminder that I was once a prisoner but now

I have been set free.

The chains that held me back have been broken, and there is nothing that can stop me now.

I need this reminder.

I need to have this picture in my head.

Because, let's be honest: it's easy to sink into despair,

into shame,

into fear or anger.

It's easy to get bound up again.

But then I remember:

Steko.

Persevere.

Stay strong.

Don't submit to the old ways.

Don't go back.

Why does Christ set us free?

For freedom's sake.

That's what Paul tells us.

Not for Jesus to show us how awesome he is and not to prove a point,

but simply so you can experience the joy in being truly free.

Freedom for the sake of freedom.

Christ has come.

You have been set free.

So fly.

Revel in your freedom.

Tower

For freedom Christ has set us free.
Stand firm, therefore, and do not submit
again to a yoke of slavery.

GALATIANS 5:1

SOMETIMES THE THINGS WE have put our trust in get tested and we find out they aren't as strong as we thought they were.

We trust in our health, in our bodies.

We trust in relationships.

We trust in our careers.

And then things happen.

We hear, "You have cancer,"

or "I don't think I want to be married anymore,"

or "I'm sorry, we're going to have to let you go,"

and suddenly we see that what we trusted wasn't so strong after all.

This psalm reminds us that there is only one strong tower.

And when life seems uncertain, when we are shaken, we can trust in the Lord.

This psalm reminds me of lighthouses that have been through centuries of storms and still stand tall.

When all else fails, when the GPS breaks and the radar system goes down, that lighthouse is still there.

Ready to go.

Standing strong and sure.

And that is God for us.

Ready and waiting.

Strong and secure.

When we put our trust in God, nothing will be able to knock us down.

Not the strongest wind, not the wildest storm.

Notice how this verse says that the righteous run to the strong tower.

Which to me implies that they were not there to begin with.

It doesn't say that the strong tower protects those who are there the whole time. It says the tower is there for those who run to it.

When all else fails.

I know you know what I'm talking about. I know you've

been there.

We try everything else and then, when all those things don't work, we go to God.

Our strong tower.

Ready and waiting.

So if you've put your trust in something else, and that trust is being rocked, know that the strong tower is waiting.

Has always been waiting.

And if you want to try a few other things, that doesn't change anything about God.

God will always be waiting.

And when the GPS fails and the radar goes out and the ground you are on seems less than solid,

run—don't walk—to the strong tower.

The one that has, is, and will always be there.

Run to God and be safe.

Omnipresent

Where can I go from your spirit?
Or where can I flee from your presence?
If I ascend to heaven, you are there;
if I make my bed in Sheol, you are there.
If I take the wings of the morning
and settle at the farthest limits of the sea,
even there your hand shall lead me,
and your right hand shall hold me fast.

PSALM 139: 7-10

IF YOU JUMP BACK a few verses in this psalm, you'll see a reminder of how God hems us in and surrounds us. It's good stuff.

But the psalmist doesn't stop there.

Instead, this poem continues with the reminder of God's presence in our lives.

And really, there isn't a day I don't need to hear this reminder.

There is always something pulling my attention away from God.

Always.

There is always good news and bad news in every day.

But that's why we have this promise:

No matter where we find ourselves, God will be there.

While this text can be interpreted in a lot of different ways, I find myself thinking of it figuratively instead of literally.

In "heaven and hell," I hear "good days and bad."

So to me, this text says: On the best of days—God is there.

And on the worst possible days—God is there.

There is no place that God can't be.

Name a place.

God is there.

Name a moment.

God is there.

God is in birthing rooms and nurseries.

God is in chemo centers and oncology wards.

God is in cars on the freeway and on couches in homes.

Heaven or hell.

Land or sea.

Near or far.

Good or bad.

God is there.

What a promise to hear today!

No matter what you are going through, no matter where you are, no matter who else is around, no matter what time of day or night, God is there.

God. Is. There.

With You

How weighty to me are your thoughts, O God!
How vast is the sum of them!
I try to count them—they are more than the sand;
I come to the end—I am still with you.

PSALM 139:17-18

IN THE STORY OF JOB, right after Job has finally let loose and yelled at God for all the pain and grief he has been enduring, God basically says to him, "Who are you?"

It seems pretty harsh, especially considering all Job has been through, and it could likely be filed under "Things Not to Say to Someone Who Is Grieving," but there is a lot of truth in this response.

We like to have the answers.

And not just have the answers, but have answers with certainty.

When someone tells us that we can't know all the answers, we think it's harsh, or mean, or simply untrue.

The psalmist today points out that God's thoughts are more numerous than the sand.

And we want to know all of them?

The hardest thing we are asked to do, I believe, is to let God be God and let us be us.

We are not God.

Theologian Paul Tillich once said, "The opposite of faith isn't doubt, it's certainty."

We can't be certain of a lot of things.

We want to know all of the answers.

But we can't. That's not real life.

We don't know what tomorrow will bring.

We don't know what today will bring.

But we do know that today and tomorrow, God is there.

Remember this same psalm, verses 7–10?

"Where can I go from your spirit?
Or where can I flee from your presence?
If I ascend to heaven, you are there;
if I make my bed in Sheol, you are there.
If I take the wings of the morning

and settle at the farthest limits of the sea,
even there your hand shall lead me,
and your right hand shall hold me fast."

No matter where you are, no matter what you are going through, when it ends—however it ends—and all along the way, God is still there.

That word there, *still*, at the end of verse 18 . . . it's a little word that means a lot.

Because it literally means "continuance."

Continuance: the state of remaining in existence.

This is what God is for you.

Still.

God is still with us.

God is in a state of remaining with us.

At the end of every day,

at the end of everything that life throws at us,

even at the end of life itself,

God is *still* with us.

God's Arms

My heart is not proud, O LORD,

my eyes are not haughty;

I do not concern myself with great matters
or things too wonderful for me.

But I have stilled and quieted my soul;

like a weaned child with its mother,

like a weaned child is my soul within me.

O Israel, put your hope in the LORD,

both now and forevermore.

PSALM 131

HAVE YOU EVER HAD one of those days where the perfect verse came up right when you needed it?

That's how this text came to me.

And I think it came to me at the perfect moment because as I read it, it felt like opposite day:

My heart is not proud?

I do not concern myself with great matters?

I have quieted my soul?

Um. Not so much.

But the images given in this psalm are so lovely, and they make my soul long for the kind of peace and stillness I read about here.

Imagine, either from your own experience or a picture in your mind, the comfort of when you were a kid, just crawling up to your mom's lap and settling in.

Not because you needed to be fed or needed anything, but because of the calm and comfort and stillness she provided.

Do you remember that?

Now, imagine, again from your own experience or or a picture in your mind, that moment of joy when your own child crawled into your lap for that same moment of peace and comfort.

Remember what it felt like to be able to provide that gift of pure, unconditional love to your son or daughter?

This lovely psalm not only tells us how God feels when we put our hope and trust in him (and we should pay attention to that part), but also reminds us how *we* could feel when we do the same thing. When you put your hope in God, things change: your soul quiets and calms, and you rest secure and loved in his arms.

I don't know about you, but my soul could use a little quieting down.

So close your eyes, and imagine being surrounded by God's arms.

Feel the love, peace, and calm that comes from being right where you are meant to be.

Joy

As the Father has loved me,
so I have loved you; abide in my love.

I have said these things to you so that
my joy may be in you, and that your joy
may be complete.

JOHN 15:9 & 11

I JUST FINISHED HOSTING a small gathering of four five-year-old girls.

Yep, just me and four littles, eating mac 'n cheese, putting on princess dresses, and dancing—so much dancing.

It was loud, and chaotic, and adorable.

It was also joyful.

If there is one thing we can learn from kids, it's how to be joyful.

Joy is different than happiness.

Happiness is a feeling.

Joy is a way of looking at the world.

It's a state of being.

It's a choice.

I think you can be sad and still be joyful.

I also think you can be happy and completely joyless.

In these two verses from John, Jesus gives us the key to joy.

And it's not even remotely related to happiness.

It's all about love.

And not just any love, but God's love.

God's love is the key to joy.

The command (not request) given to us by Jesus here in these verses is to sit secure in that love.

Abide in it, he tells us.

When you do that, you'll have joy, and not just any joy, but *complete* joy.

Who doesn't want that?

I like to imagine what it might look like to abide in the love of God.

Maybe it's like cozying up in your favorite blanket on a cold night, or getting a huge hug from someone warm and a lot bigger than you. Maybe it's like looking up at the sky on a clear night and seeing nothing but stars.

Abiding in God's love feels like being surrounded by warmth and love.

When we stay close to God, we can't help but experience love.

And when we stay close to God, abiding there, what comes next is joy.

Not the fleeting feeling of happiness, but deep, rich, warm, peaceful joy.

You are beloved.

Beloved.

Remember that today.

Abide in that. Stay with that thought for a long while. Let it surround you with warmth and love.

Joy will most surely follow.

Storms

The disciples woke Jesus and said to him,
"Teacher, don't you care if we drown?"

Jesus got up, rebuked the wind, and said to
the waves, "Quiet, be still!"

Then the wind died down and it was
completely calm.

MARK 4:38-39

HAVE YOU EVER BEEN in a storm (real or metaphorical)
that was so chaotic and scary that you weren't sure if you'd
make it through?

How often in those storms have we called out, just like the
disciples, "Jesus, don't you care? Look at me! I'm drowning
over here!"

I've noticed that I can work myself into a frenzy about
storms pretty quickly.

I watch the horizon for darkening sky.

I hover near windows and look at approaching clouds.

In the middle of storms, I watch the radar closely and constantly listen for sirens and alerts.

Can't be too careful, right?

I can make the storm feel worse than it is, seeing only the things that could go wrong and creating hopeless scenarios in my mind.

So I love this story. Because I'm right there with the disciples in that boat.

Freaking out.

Maybe even working myself into a panic.

And that is not to say that there aren't things worthy of panic.

I mean, the storm in the sea around the disciples' boat was really bad.

They really did think they weren't going to make it through.

So Jesus got up and calmed the storm.

And we could stop there. I mean, that's the point of the story, right?

Just call on God and he will calm the storm in your life.

I know you've heard that before.

But I actually think this verse is about something more.

It's not just about God calming storms of life, though that

can and does happen.

It is also about trusting God even in the midst of those storms.

Even when the boat looks like it's about to go under.

Jesus looks to his disciples after calming the storm and asks them why they didn't have faith.

They don't answer, but we know it's because they were scared.

They thought the storm was more powerful than God.

They couldn't believe Jesus was sleeping through it.

Jesus wanted the trust of his disciples.

He wanted them to remember that he would keep them safe even when things looked dire.

After all, even in the storm, Jesus didn't leave the boat.

He was there the whole time—calm, relaxed, secure in knowing who was in charge and who was bigger than the waves.

So the next time you feel like you're in the midst of a storm of massive proportions,

when you think the ship is about to go down,

remember that God is in the boat with you, and there is *no* storm bigger or more powerful than God.

Worth the Wait

I consider that the sufferings of this
present time are not worth comparing with the
glory about to be revealed to us.

For the creation waits with eager longing
for the revealing of the children of God;

for the creation was subjected to futility, not of its own
will but by the will of the one who subjected it,

in hope that the creation itself will be set free from its
bondage to decay and will obtain the freedom of the
glory of the children of God.

ROMANS 8:18–21

MANY OF US HAVE heard or read Romans 8 at some
point in our lives—maybe when we were going through
difficult times—because it contains the huge and comforting
promises of verses 35–39. They remind us, quite clearly, that
there is nothing that can separate us from God's love.

Nothing.

Not health.

Not sickness.

Not good times.

Not bad times.

Nothing.

Since Romans 8 ends so wonderfully, we often jump ahead to those closing verses, the part we love so much, to immerse ourselves in that promise when we need it most.

But when we do that, we miss the amazingness that comes earlier.

Verses 18–21 tell us that something is coming.

Something bigger and better than anything we are going through right now.

In *The Message: The Bible in Contemporary Language,* author Eugene Peterson paraphrases these verses:

"This is why I don't think there's any comparison between the present hard times and the coming good times. The created world itself can hardly wait for what's coming next." [1]

God is at work in the world. Right now.

And the created world can hardly wait for what God is doing.

---

1 Peterson, Eugene. *The Message: The Bible in Contemporary Language.* Colorado Springs, CO: NavPress, 2003, p2044

So we, too, wait for God's work to be completed.

Even though waiting is hard, there is something joyful in our anticipation.

Again, in *The Message*, Paul writes that our waiting is like a pregnant mother:

"That is why the waiting does not diminish us, any more than waiting diminishes a pregnant mother. We are enlarged in the waiting. We don't see what is enlarging us. But the longer we wait, the larger we become, and the more joyful our expectancy."[2]

God is working in you too.

Right now.

It's true.

And like the rest of the world, we also wait for God's work to be completed.

It's hard to wait.

It's hard to be in pain, or sick, or going through something really difficult.

But we can trust that God is at work.

To be clear—God is not making you sick, or causing your pain, or making you go through something difficult—but

---

2 Peterson, Eugene. *The Message: The Bible in Contemporary Language.* Colorado Springs, CO: NavPress, 2003, p2044

God is at work within that experience.

Making it something new.

Making you new.

And while God works, we wait.

Because when it's done, when that work is complete, we won't even be able to handle the awesomeness.

In the meantime, we hold tightly to those promises at the end of Romans 8.

Nothing can come between you and God.

Nothing.

God at Work

But Joseph said to them, "Don't be afraid.
Am I in the place of God?

You intended to harm me, but God intended
it for good to accomplish what is now being
done, the saving of many lives."

GENESIS 50:19-20

ONE OF MY FAVORITE seminary professors says these are
some of the most important verses in all of Genesis.

That's a big statement, considering Genesis contains
creation and Noah and Abraham and covenants all over the
place.

So what makes these verses such a big deal? Especially since
we do not read them as regularly as others in the book?

These two verses tell us something huge about God:
even when he seems hard to find, God is working.

Let me say that again:

even when God seems hard to find, God is working.

No matter what the scenario, God is working in it.

But—and this is important—

God doesn't make the bad things happen, but he *is* working in them.

Notice how Joseph doesn't say that God made bad things happen. He said his brothers *intended* something bad, and it was the actions of God in the midst of the bad stuff that made good happen.

Does that mean Joseph's being left behind and sold into slavery magically became good?

No.

Not even close. Being sold by your jealous brothers is a difficult thing to make good.

Does that mean Joseph was okay with all that had happened to him?

Nope.

He forgave his brothers, but what happened was never okay.

But did God work within the bad?

Yes.

So much yes.

I know that trust is sometimes hard.

I imagine while Joseph was sitting at the bottom of an old well or in jail in Egypt, it was hard for him to trust.

But in those times when Joseph felt like God had forgotten him, God was hard at work.

So if there is bad happening in your life right now, trust that God is in it.

Even when it's hard to see God in your life, trust that God is there.

Deep within what is hard, working to make good things happen.

God is there.

God. Is. There.

And God is at work.

This Far

> Then Samuel took a stone and set it up
> between Mizpah and Shen.
>
> He named it Ebenezer, saying, 'Thus far
> has the Lord helped us.'
>
> 1 SAMUEL 7:12

ISRAEL HAD JUST ENGAGED in battle with the terrible Philistines and won.

This was a big deal, because Israel knew they only won because of the help of God.

So Samuel took a stone and set it on the ground to mark the spot where they had received God's help. Then, when the Israelites looked back at that stone, they could remember that they got to that point because of God.

Ebenezer means stone of help in Hebrew. I think we all have our own Ebenezers we can raise today.

You might be going through something difficult right now, but you are not alone.

God is with you right now.

You are still here, still fighting, still strong.

Maybe you've come through something difficult and have come out victorious, just like the Israelites, and you know you are where you are because God was with you through it.

So today, right now, it's Ebenezer time.

If you can, find a rock, grab a Sharpie, and write on it.

Write where you have come from, what you have triumphed over, or where you see God.

And then place that stone somewhere where you can see it often, where you can look at it and be reminded of how far you've come.

If rock-writing isn't your thing, then get a journal and write it down.

If you want to be artsy, draw it.

But today, together, we're going to raise our Ebenezers.

As the old hymns sings:

"Here I raise my Ebenezer

hither by thy help I've come."

That's us. Here, raising our stones of help to recognize how God is working and helping in our lives.

If you feel like it, take a picture and share it on Twitter or Instagram and Facebook with #TeamUplift #UpliftEbenezer.

Raise 'em up!

New Songs

Sing to the Lord a new song;
sing to the Lord all the earth.

Sing to the Lord, praise his name;
proclaim his salvation day after day.

PSALM 96: 1-2

I'VE BEEN THINKING A BIT about the phrase "sing a new song" a lot lately. For some reason it seems to be everywhere I look.

The phrase "sing a new song" is in five psalms other than Psalm 96, and is used a few times in both Isaiah and Revelation. So it's not an uncommon phrase, but that doesn't mean I don't have a lot of questions about it.

What does it mean to sing a new song?

How do I do it?

What makes a song new?

Do I have to go around writing new songs all the time?

Can I use someone else's new song?

And what was wrong with my old one?

The important part of this phrase isn't the singing, or even the song. The important part is "new."

In Hebrew, new is chadash (pronounced ha-desh). Chadash means "new," or a "new thing," or even "fresh."

I like that: fresh.

Sometimes we get in ruts.

We keep singing the same old songs.

We go through each day doing the same things and feeling the same ways in our work and in our relationships.

Just think about it. Most likely your day is full of routine: get up, eat breakfast, drive to work, work, drive home, make dinner, eat, hang out, or watch television, or read, go to bed.

How often are your worries about health and wealth and relationships as routine?

New day, same worries.

Today we are being called to try a new song.

To sing something fresh.

To try thinking and acting and feeling things that are not the same old same old.

To sing new songs in our daily lives and relationships and in our faith, too.

But first you have to answer a question. What is your old song?

You can't sing a new one unless you're honest about the one that you are currently singing.

Once you know the answer to that, ask yourself what it might look like to change the song you are singing.

If this is difficult for you—if you are trying and getting frustrated because you can't think of a new song—try remembering this:

you are a child of God.

Try this as the lens through which to look at your day.

Try it out as the melody that anchors your new song.

And then sing. Sing that new song today.

Take a fresh look at the life you have.

The body you've been given.

The people you love.

The grace that has saved you.

The faith that keeps you.

It's time to break out of the routine and try something new.

Sing a new song.

Morning

Let the morning bring me word
of your unfailing love, for I have put my
trust in you.

Show me the way I should go, for
to you I entrust my life.

PSALM 143:8

THERE IS SOMETHING SACRED about the morning.

Let me be clear in saying I haven't ever really been a
morning person, ever.

To be honest, I love to sleep more than almost anything else.

But when I became a parent, I quickly had to learn to
embrace the morning.

Predawn feedings have turned into busy mornings spent
trying to get to the bus stop on time with a dressed and fed
child.

Mornings can be chaos.

Still—and I never thought I'd say this—I have found the sacred in the beginning of each new day.

Day after day, I find myself getting up before everyone else.

Early mornings have become the calm before the storm, the peace before the chaos.

And I have learned to love those moments of stillness and quiet that morning brings.

I watch the sun slowly rise, and I offer up my day to God.

Scripture is full of these same early morning moments.

Examples are not hard to find.

I think this is because mornings can represent what God does for us in our lives.

Each day is new.

Each day is a new start, a new beginning.

This is what mornings do for our lives.

Each morning we have the chance to let go of yesterday—of things past—and welcome the new day.

Each time the sun rises, we watch light overtaking the darkness,

and we are reminded that this is what God does for us.

Each new day we can be reminded of the love God has for us; reminded that each day is a gift, and that no matter how dark things get, the light will always come.

Our God is a God of light.

Our God is a God of morning.

So tomorrow, get up before the sun.

Sit with your coffee or tea or juice or water, watch the new day come, and see it for what it really is: a sacred moment,

a reminder of God's abounding love and grace coming once again, making all things new.

Step by Step

Our steps are made firm by the Lord,
and he delights in our way;

though we stumble, we shall not
fall headlong, for the Lord holds us
by the hand.

PSALM 37:23-24

OH, I LOVE THIS section of Psalm 37!

The very first words remind us that God walks alongside us, delighting in each step we take.

Isn't that a lovely image?

Every time we take a step, God is delighted by it.

God is not ambivalently watching you. God is *delighted* by you.

Think of this image the next time you go for a walk or are about to start something new.

God is delighting in you.

Then, as if that weren't good enough, the psalm goes on to say that no matter how difficult it may be to take the next step, even if that next step makes us trip and lose our balance, we will not fall, because God is with us.

Notice the words here. They don't say, "If we stumble." They say, "Though we stumble."

The Hebrew here is כִּי (prounounced ki), which can mean "when" or "for."

Yep. This text says, "When we stumble."

Not if.

When.

It's going to happen.

So the question when we are on our faith journey and on our daily walk of life isn't, "What happens if I stumble?"

The question is, "What happens *when* I stumble?"

This is an important distinction because it changes how we look at stumbling.

If you are anything like me, you usually equate stumbling with failing.

I get frustrated when I don't understand something, or when I have doubts, or when I am struggling with how or what I believe.

When life doesn't go my way, when I feel like I've taken a misstep or tripped up and lost my balance, I see it as a weakness, as a failing.

But stumbling is a part of the process.

It's going to happen. Not if, but when.

And instead of seeing it as failing, I can teach myself to see it differently.

Not only as a way to learn and grow but as a way to see God's presence.

Because when we stumble—not if, but when—God has promised to be there.

Look at verse 24.

We stumble, and there God is.

Holding us by the hand.

Making sure we don't hit the ground.

You know that moment when you're holding a child's hand and they trip and start to fall, so you just grab on a little tighter and get them back on their feet?

God is doing that very thing for you.

So if you feel like you're stumbling today, know you are not alone.

God has your hand and will make sure you don't fall.

And then, when you take that next step a little more steadily, God delights again.

In you.

Walk on, dear friends.

God's Time

But do not forget this one thing, dear friends: with the Lord a day is like thousand years, and a thousand years are like a day.

The Lord is not slow in keeping his promise, as some understand slowness.

He is patient with you, not wanting anyone to perish, but everyone to come to repentance.

2 PETER 3:8-9

HAVE YOU EVER FELT like time is moving too fast?

Or have you ever felt like it couldn't possibly go any slower?

When our little was still new, someone told me, "The days are long but the years are short."

Oh, that felt so true. It still feels true.

In parenthood, yes, but also in dark and difficult days.

We often look at life in increments:

six weeks of this, two of that;

six months until the next test, treatment, scan;

one year until the next season, stage of life.

And sometimes those increments can seem slow.

When we pray, the answers can seem to take forever to come as well.

Sometimes it seems like they don't come at all!

Peter was writing to a group of people who were wondering when Jesus was going to come and fulfill the promise he made to them.

They thought it was taking forever for him to return.

But Peter knew better.

Slow isn't bad.

And time isn't either.

Time is a gift.

God is not slow to keep his promises,

but what he gives us is time. Lots of time.

Time to live our lives.

To be fully present right where we are.

To stop looking to the next thing.

Time to love those around us.

Time to turn back to God, even when we don't understand everything that is happening.

God is patient with our frustrations because he wants to give us as much time as we need to come to him. And sometimes, it takes a lot of time for that to happen.

So when things seem slow—

when it seems like all you're doing is waiting,

or counting down the time between one thing and another—

know, without a doubt,

that God has promised to be with you.

And because we know God keeps his promises, we know God is with you now.

Right now.

In the waiting.

In the slowness.

In the mundaneness.

In it all.

God. Is. With. You.

Chosen

But you are not like that,
for you are a chosen people.

You are royal priests, a holy nation,
God's very own possession.

As a result, you can show others the
goodness of God, for he called you out of
the darkness into his wonderful light.

1 PETER 2:9

HAVE YOU EVER HAD one of those days where you
weren't sure who you were?

A day where you started to believe the messages around you
in the world that tell you over and over that you aren't good
enough?

That you are too much, or too little, or you need more, or
need less?

Messages that call you bad instead of good and unlovable
instead of beloved?

These messages are everywhere.

All. The. Time.

So yeah, it's kind of impossible to avoid those days in which we sink into doubt.

It's on those days that I need this good word from Peter.

Peter who doubted and stumbled and followed and denied.

Peter who heard messages from others and didn't always believe either.

But in this verse, Peter steps in to remind us just who we are.

Whose we are.

"You aren't any of those things," he says. "You are chosen."

And if that isn't clear enough for you, he goes on. "You are God's own possession."

I need this promise all the time.

As often as I hear things that are opposite, I need to hear this.

I am a part of God's family.

He chose me.

Me.

I needed this promise so much that I literally made it a permanent part of my body:

My right wrist has the word "beloved" tattooed on it.

I am a beloved child of God.

Every time I see that word on my wrist I am reminded of who I am and whose I am.

And you know what? God chose you too.

Yep, you.

You are God's beloved child.

Remind yourself of that right now.

Say it out loud (really).

God chose me.

All those messages we hear that aren't true?

They are darkness.

And the promise that Peter reminds us of today, that we are God's chosen, claimed, beloved children?

That is light.

God is constantly and consistently calling us out of darkness and into light.

And it's wonderful.

Knocking

Here I am! I stand at the door and knock.
If anyone hears my voice and opens the
door, I will come in and eat with him,
and he with me.

REVELATION 3:20

THE LUTHERAN PART OF me cringes when I first read this verse.

I struggle with the idea that God's presence in our lives requires some action on our part.

First we have to hear, and then we have to open the door?

That seems like a lot of pressure to put on myself.

How will I know what to listen for?

What if I miss it?

What if I can't find the door?

But focusing on the hearing and opening is missing the point of this short but well-known verse.

Because this verse is not, at its foundation, about us. It's about Christ.

It's about the length of time Christ is willing to stand and knock.

It's actually about how far Christ is willing to go for us.

When translated from the Greek, this verse says, "Behold, I stand, I have stood for a long time, and I am still standing and will continue to stand and knock."

This is a verse not about *your* action, but about *Christ's persistence* in your life.

No matter what, Christ is not going to stop knocking at your heart.

No matter what doubts you have, no matter what questions spring up, no matter how often you ignore God's call in your life, Christ is never going to stop trying.

The love of God is always there.

Always.

Whether it's inside my heart or outside is up to me, but either way it's still there.

Even when we give up on God, when we lock him out, God never gives up on us.

There's great comfort in that for me.

God is like home.

Always there.

Always available.

Always ready.

Even when I'm not.

So it's not about me at all.

Thank goodness.

Pray

Likewise the Spirit helps us in
our weakness;

for we do not know how to pray as we
ought, but that very Spirit intercedes with
sighs too deep for words.

And God, who searches the heart, knows
what is the mind of the Spirit,

because the Spirit intercedes for the saints
according to the will of God.

ROMANS 8:26–27

OUT OF ALL THE questions of faith, one of the most
common themes is prayer.

How are we supposed to pray?

Why do we pray?

What if I don't feel like praying?

What if I don't do it right?

Have you ever felt this way?

In our faith life, just as everywhere else, we have highs and lows.

We have times in which our prayers just come.

They happen naturally, easily, and with a grace of words we didn't know we had.

But then then there are all the other days.

We're in a dark place,

or we're sick,

or we're tired,

or we had the worst day,

and then suddenly the prayers don't come quite as easily.

It's on those days that I like to have the reminder given in this verse.

It is on our weakest days, the days where we are struggling under the weight of life, that the Spirit says,

"I got this,"

and takes the messy, exhausted, incomprehensible jumble of our thoughts and gives them to God.

And God hears them.

Even when they aren't words at all, God hears.

Even when our prayers don't come, God hears.

Even when we don't have it all together. God hears.

God hears our prayers.

So no matter if your prayers are flowing today or if you are in the midst of a day without the words,

God still hears you.

You can pray today. Right now.

No matter what you are going through or where your heart is or what you're feeling,

Prayer is always possible and God will always hear you.

That's the heart-filling, worry-relieving promise in these verses today.

You don't need to be perfect or have the perfect prayer to be heard.

And if you have the words today, if things are feeling good and freely flowing, then I urge you to pray. Part of being a part of a community and #TeamUplift is praying for each other.

Because even though your day isn't so bad, someone in your life or in this community right now is having a day that is not so great, a day when the words are not coming and they feel like words might not ever come.

So we need you to pray.

Pray for this community, pray for your loved ones, pray for yourself, pray for the world and those in it that you don't know at all.

Just pray.

Laughter

For everything there is a season, and a
time for every matter under heaven . . .

A time to weep and a time to laugh, and
time to mourn and a time to dance.

ECCLESIASTES 3:1 & 4

I READ A STATISTIC the other day that said kids laugh an average of four hundred times a day.

Four hundred.

That's a giggle every 3.6 minutes.

If you take into account sleeping, it averages to a belly laugh every 1.8 minutes.

But adults?

They laugh only an average of four times a day.

Four!

Factor in sleeping and that averages to only one laugh every four hours.

This is not okay.

In fact, this simply astounded me: the low number for adults and, even more, the shocking discrepancy between adults and kids.

And I hope you'll agree that something has got to change.

It is not always that fun to be an adult, so we let it be not fun.

It's just easier to find things to be annoyed at, or mad about, or heartbroken over.

And when we focus on those things, it's easy to only laugh four times a day.

This is why we regularly look to kids as reminders of how to live life to the fullest and with great joy.

To have a heart of joy in an adult world is hard.

But it's possible.

Joy is a choice.

It's not like happiness.

Happiness is something you have, but it is completely dependent on the external situation.

Joy is something you choose.

It is dependent only on you.

Even when there are things that annoy you or frustrate you or drain you of your energy, you can still choose joy.

Even when it feels impossible, you can—I promise you can—choose joy.

Author and speaker Brené Brown once said, "The root of joy is gratitude."[3]

People often assume that joy causes us to be grateful, but it's really the other way around.

Gratefulness leads us into joy.

And joy comes out in laughter.

So today, no matter what kind of day you are having,

no matter what news you've received,

no matter how you are feeling,

no matter where you are,

take some time for gratitude.

You are loved.

You are here.

Be grateful

---

3 Brown, Brene'. "The Power of Vulnerability" TED. June 2010. Lecture

not just for the obvious, big things—faith, family, friends–
but the small things too.
The way the rain makes the leaves stick to the ground.
The way your first sip of coffee tastes like heaven itself.
The way your couch and blankets beckon on a cool fall day.

"It is not joy that makes us grateful;
it is gratitude that makes us joyful."[4]

There is a time for everything—and today is a time for joy.

And let's up our laughter average today too, while we're at it.

---

4 Brown, Brene'. "The Power of Vulnerability" TED. June 2010.
Lecture

Enough

In Christ Jesus the whole structure
is joined together and grows into
a holy temple in the Lord;

in whom you also are built together
spiritually into a dwelling place for God.

EPHESIANS 2:21

I HAVE A SIGN hanging on the wall to the right of my desk that says, "You are always enough."

I think the great injustice of our culture is that it has caused a drought of worthiness.

We are surrounded, bombarded even, by voices and pictures and words telling us we are not enough.

And if we want to be enough we need to change.

We need more stuff,

more technology,

more "likes,"

more muscle,

more friends,

more posts . . . more more more.

And as we're constantly surrounded by all those messages, we start to agree with them.

We think we aren't enough.

We think that we need something else to make us worthy.

We end up being pretty hard on ourselves.

In his words above, the apostle Paul is talking about our place in the family of God. The structure he refers to as the "household of God."

And it is our place in that family—our identity as beloved children of God—that makes us something holy.

A dwelling place for God.

Yeah, you read that right.

You.

You are God's dwelling place.

Think about what that means!

God dwells in you.

It's not what you do, or look like, or weigh, or make, that gives you worth.

It is God's dwelling in you that declares you are enough.

You are a holy place.

You are beautiful, and you are enough.

When you were baptized, a cross was placed on your forehead, and you were called and claimed as a child of God.

You were enough.

You are still enough.

So today, when you find yourself tempted to believe that you are not enough, remember that cross on your head.

Take your finger and trace that cross again.

Remember what it means.

Child of God, you have been sealed by the Holy Spirit and marked with the cross of Christ forever.

That is who you are.

And you are enough.

You are always enough.

Known

The Lord said to Moses, "My presence will go with you, and I will give you rest."

And Moses said, "If your presence will not go, do not carry us up from here. For how shall it be known that I have found favor in your sight, I and your people, unless you go with us? In this way, we shall be distinct, I and your people, from every people on the face of the earth."

The Lord said to Moses, "I will do the very thing that you have asked; for you have found favor in my sight, and I know you by name."

EXODUS 33:14–17

HAVE YOU EVER HAD that moment of doubt in which you believe that God's promises are just too good to be true?

You hear God say, "I am going with you" and you wonder, "Really? Because it doesn't feel like it."

You're not alone.

These verses today from Exodus remind us of the reality of our doubt and God's response to it.

And it starts with Moses.

Moses, the guy who led the Israelites out of slavery. That Moses.

He doubted God's promise too.

And the way Moses doubts is pretty great.

He basically gives God an out, saying, "Look, God, if you decide you can't go with us, then don't bring us out of here. It's cool if you can't, God, we get it. You're busy and stuff, but we just need to know you're really with us before we go. I mean, how do we know if we're really yours unless you're with us?"

Now, one might expect God to lay the smackdown on Moses a bit.

Right?

We expect God to say, "Come on, Moses! Haven't I done enough to show you I'm with you? That I'm on your side? Remember the plagues? The parting of the Red Sea? The manna and quail in the desert and the water from the rock? Remember? How can you even say I'm not with you? What do I have to do?"

But that's not God.

God just says, "Yep. I'm with you.

I'm with you. Just as you asked. Because I love you, I know

you, and you are mine."

God knows us.

God knows we doubt the promises.

God knows we go through hard days, weeks, months, and start to wonder whether God might really, truly be with us.

God knows that sometimes we are really struggling and just have to ask, "Are you with me, God?"

And with us, as with Moses, God doesn't take us on a trip down memory lane through all the ways he has been with us over the years.

Nope—God just looks at us with love, and says, "Yep. I'm really with you."

Notice what God says will happen when he is with us.

"My presence will go with you and I will give you rest."

The result of trusting God is rest.

We can stop worrying.

We can stop asking God to be with us, and just rest.

God is with us.

God loves you and knows you.

Doubts and all.

You belong to God.

So where else would God be?

So go ahead.

Ask God to be with you again today.

The response is always the same: "Yep. I'm with you."

Unshakable

For God alone my soul waits in silence;
from him comes my salvation.

He alone is my rock and my salvation, my
fortress; I shall never be shaken.

PSALM 62:1-2

I'VE BEEN SHAKEN MANY times in my life.

I have had weeks where things looked really bleak and it felt like the darkness might actually be winning.

There were days where I questioned whether or not God was really in it with me.

I know you've been there.

How can we not have been there?

Life is hard.

And dark.

And did I say hard?

So I get shaken, and I confess, I don't often wait in silence.

I'm a verbal processor, and on top of that, I often find myself unable to sit silently when someone is saying things that I think are just wrong.

Then, this morning, I read a letter from Alfred Delp, a Jesuit priest, written while he was imprisoned in Germany in 1945 for opposing Hitler. He wrote, "There is perhaps nothing we modern people need more than to be genuinely shaken up. Where life is firm we need to sense its firmness; and where it is unstable and uncertain and has no basis, no foundation, we need to know this, too." [5]

I think sometimes we've been told that when we put our trust in the wrong things, then God comes and messes them up.

We trust in money, we lose a job.

We trust in our health, we get sick.

We trust in leaders, we find them to be corrupt.

We trust in relationships, they get broken.

These things happen every day and someone inevitably comes forward and says that God is doing this so that we remember to trust in him.

Ugh.

No.

No no no no no.

---

5 Delp, Alfred. *"The Shaking Reality of Advent" from Watch for the Light: Readings for Advent and Christmas.* Plough Publishing House. 2001. p82.

What kind of God does that?

Not the God that I believe in.

So this letter from Alfred Delp stopped me in my tracks because it's so different than thinking God is responsible for shaking things up.

It's not that God comes and stirs the pot and causes tragedy to make a point.

No way.

It's not God at all. It's the other stuff.

All those things I trusted weren't God.

So they fail.

They crumble.

Because that's what things that aren't God do.

Things that aren't God fail. Plain and simple.

These verses and quote make me realize how often I choose to stand on other things and hope for stability.

Things that aren't God.

And those things crumble.

When tragedy strikes, my foundation will either be God or not.

So my foundation will either be firm or not.

But here's the good news.

No matter what I choose, no matter if I choose God or not, God chooses me.

God makes the ground beneath my feet firm.

And when God is my firm foundation, my rock, I will never be shaken.

Never.

And I don't know about you, but I could use some of that solid ground right about now.

That shake-proof foundation.

So let's stand together, on God—our unshakeable foundation.

Staying Power

When Mary reached the place
where Jesus was and saw him, she fell
at his feet and said,

"Lord, if you had been here, my brother
would not have died."

When Jesus saw her weeping, and those
with her also weeping, he was deeply
moved and troubled.

JOHN 11:32-33

WHEN THINGS ARE CONFUSING, unstable, and
unsteady—what do we do?

When we get bad news or have bad days, what question do
we ask first?

I think, honestly, our first reaction is the same as Mary's in
these verses.

Where are you, God?

Earlier in this same chapter, Martha, Mary's sister, says the
same thing. "God, if you had been here, this wouldn't have

happened."

Some of the most honest and real emotions in grief are blame and anger.

But they aren't the emotions we're comfortable with.

Tears aren't too bad, but mostly we like to jump quickly to being "fine" or "okay."

We don't want to burden our friends and family with how we're really doing and how we're really feeling.

I know you know what I'm talking about.

But this doesn't fit with what God wants for us.

In the scene above we see Jesus with Mary and Martha, grieving right alongside them at the loss of their brother.

I often find myself reminding people that they can only be where they are, and the best thing they can do is feel what they feel, when they feel it.

If you're happy, be happy.

If you're scared, be scared.

If you're angry, be angry.

Those feelings are real. And they are honest.

The short verse "Jesus wept" comes right after Jesus sees the sisters and their family grieving, and it tells us something about God that we cannot ignore.

God will not leave us alone with our emotions.

God does not leave us alone, period.

When we're grieving, God is right there with us.

When we need a minute to be angry and yell, God is there, too.

Jesus didn't leave Mary and Martha despite their anger, their blame, their confusion, and their grief.

And he won't leave you either.

Weakness

But the Lord said to me, "My grace is sufficient for you, for my power is made perfect in weakness."

Therefore I will boast all the more gladly about my weakness, so that Christ's power may rest on me.

2 CORINTHIANS 12:9

WEAKNESS.

Boy, do we have a thing against weakness.

Our culture idolizes strength.

We have saying after saying lifting up the importance of being strong.

"Pain is just weakness leaving the body."

"Only the strong survive."

And it's not just physical strength we love, but emotional strength as well.

When people lose loved ones or go through difficult times

without showing emotion, others say, "Oh, they are so strong."

I call shenanigans on this idea that strength is number one.

SHENANIGANS.

And I've got a little Biblical truth on my side.

In his Second Letter to the Corinthians, Paul brings forward one of the many paradoxes of the Gospel (Gospel = good news):

God is found in our weak places.

There are a lot of things that make me feel weak.

I'm not the strongest gal in the neighborhood, emotionally or physically.

But I'm okay with that.

Because it is precisely those places where I am weak that require me to do things that are pure Gospel-bringing.

When I am weak, I have to ask for help.

It's not the easiest thing to do, but it does create space for God and others to come in and show love.

God's power is made clear in weak places.

It's hard to admit weakness.

But it's important.

Admitting these weak places—"boasting" in them, as Paul says—is important.

Because it is through these moments of sharing that we can hear the greatest two words in the English language: me too.

Me too.

When you tell someone you love that you are struggling, you offer a chance for them to show you love or to even say "me too." A shared burden is lighter. I don't know why it works that way, but it does.

"Me too."

This is the core of the Gospel.

You feel weak in your body? Spirit? Soul?

Jesus has experienced all of this, and looks at us with love in his eyes and says, "Me too."

You aren't alone in those weak places, and even more than that: it is precisely in those weak places where there is room for Christ to come in and show you what strength looks like.

Your weak places are where grace is found, so don't be ashamed of them.

Open them up and let Christ in.

God's power is made perfect right there, in you.

Deliverance

I sought the Lord, and he answered me; he
delivered me from all my fears.

PSALM 34:4

HOW OFTEN DO WE think we have our lives under control?

How often do we think we can do it all on our own?

And then something happens. We get sick, or someone we
love dies, and we are so quickly reminded that we are not in
control, that we don't have it all together, and we cannot do
it alone.

Have you been there?

Are you there right now?

Hear me today when I say you don't have to be alone.

You are not alone.

We don't go through life and death and everything in
between alone.

How do I know this?

Because God has promised us that we will never be alone.

Promised.

For goodness' sake, we call Jesus "God with us."

God has come and has promised to never leave us on our own.

He delivers us from all our fears, from all the things that break us down.

That promise means something.

And yet, we have all reached that moment,

our breaking point,

where we realize that we simply can't do it anymore.

We're done.

Done.

You know what I mean.

German theologian Dietrich Bonhoeffer wrote this prayer in just such a moment.

"O God, early in the morning I cry to you.

Help me to pray and to concentrate my thoughts on you;

I cannot do this alone.

In me there is darkness, but with you there is light.

I am lonely, but you do not leave me.

I am feeble in heart, but with you there is help.

I am restless, but with you there is peace.

In me there is bitterness, but with you there is patience.

I do not understand your ways, but you know the way for me." [6]

Stunning, isn't it?

The whole prayer is incredible on its own, but it is even more powerful when you realize he wrote it from Flossenbürg concentration camp in Germany during World War II.

Even from that darkest of dark places, Bonhoeffer was somehow able to hold tightly to the promise of the presence of God and what that meant for him.

Notice how different God is from us in this prayer.

We are darkness, loneliness, weakness, restlessness; we are bitter and confused.

God is light, help, peace, patience, and presence.

No wonder Bonhoeffer used the words, "I cannot do this alone."

We need the reminder that God is with us, helping us to focus our thoughts on him and what he brings to us in the darkest moments.

So wherever you are dark today,

wherever you are weak, or tired, or sad, or confused, or anxious, or angry, or bitter, or restless, remember this:

God is the opposite of all those things.

---

6 Bonhoeffer, Dietrich. Prayer. From *All Will Be Well: A Gathering of Healing Prayer*. Augsburg Fortress. 1998. p123.

And God is with you.

Right now, with you.

Say the prayer of Bonhoeffer today.

You are not alone. God is with you.

It is a promise.

Breathe

The Spirit of God has made me, the breath
of the Almighty gives me life.

JOB 33:4

THERE ARE SO MANY references to breath in Scripture.
They begin right away in Genesis 1 with, "The breath of
God hovered over the darkness," continue into the New
Testament when Jesus appears to his disciples and breathes
on them, and go all the way through to Revelation as the
breath of life fills and renews creation.

The words for breath—*pneuma* (nooma) in Greek, *ruach* (roo-
ach) in Hebrew—are used interchangeably with spirit or
Holy Spirit.

This translation is not a mistake.

There is a lot of great and complex theology wrapped
around the idea of breath and spirit being the same word,

but today I'd like to simplify it a bit.

Take a deep breath in.

Now breathe out.

Again: deep breath in, long exhalation out.

That? That breathing thing you just did?

That's God.

God with you.

God in you.

In John 14:26, when Jesus left the disciples, he said that he wasn't leaving them alone but with a helper, the Holy Spirit (pneuma), who would be with them forever.

And how do we know the Spirit is with us?

We breathe.

In and out.

All day long.

All night long.

I have found it to be a great comfort to know these words are essentially the same.

This is one of the reasons that I enjoy yoga so much. Yoga is an intentional focus on the breath, which for me is a constant and intentional reminder of God within.

This works in other places too: when going on walks or runs, taking quiet time, or even just taking ten seconds for a deep breath or two.

No matter where you are, what you are going through, what is around you,

when you need to know where God is, all you have to do is breathe.

The breath of the Almighty gives me life.

A few more times. Breathe in deeply. And let it out.

God with us.

God with you.

"The breath of the Almighty gives me life."

PS: If you breathe a cycle of deep breaths in and out fifteen times, the body stops producing cortisol, the stress hormone, and makes endorphins, the happy hormone, instead. And that can last up to an hour! That means a short few minutes of breathing can calm you down and make you feel better. Science!

Mighty

The Lord your God is with you,
he is mighty to save.

He will take great delight in you, he will
quiet you with his love, he will rejoice over
you with singing.

ZEPHANIAH 3:17

I SIMPLY LOVE THIS VERSE. You may recognize the lyrics
if you've been at a band-led worship service in the past
ten years or so, but it's a stunning verse, just packed full of
promises.

And I mean really full. Just look at them all!

God is with you.

God will save you.

God delights in you.

God loves you.

God rejoices with you.

Everyone should memorize this verse, because there is not a day in which we don't need at least one of the promises in it.

Promise #1: The Lord your God is with you.

God is with you, all the time and in every circumstance.

You are not alone.

That promise by itself is pretty awesome, but God doesn't stop there.

Promise #2: God is mighty to save.

There is nothing that God can't redeem.

There is nothing bigger than God. That's why the word "mighty" is used here. God is big.

God is bigger than any cancer, any sickness, any heartache, any grief, any difficulty.

God is mighty to save.

Then, as if that weren't good enough, there is Promise #3: God delights in you.

God loves you so much he can't help but be delighted by what you do.

You know how people go all mushy over babies and puppies? That's God delighting in you. When God looks at you and sees a beloved child, he is delighted.

And then Promise #4: God will quiet you with his love.

When you are in full-on panic mode,

when your anxiety has reached a level that is almost not doable, think of how much God loves you and let it quiet you. The love of God—love that is bigger than anything—covers you and brings you peace. What a promise!

And last but not least, Promise #5: God is rejoicing over you with singing.

You know how sometimes you hear a song and it just perfectly describes how you're feeling even when plain old words just can't? Yeah. God too.

God loves you so much that he breaks into song.

All those promises.

Promises everywhere today.

Hear them, feel them, trust them.

Listening

I love the Lord, for he heard my voice; he
heard my cry for mercy.

Because he turned his ear to me, I will call
on him as long as I live.

PSALM 116:1-2

PSALM 116 IS A PSALM that I recommend reading in its
entirety.

It's a song of rescue and healing and trust in the midst of
fear, and who doesn't need that?

The first two verses are about God and how God hears us.

I think we all know deep down this is true, but sometimes I
think we forget to talk to God in the first place.

When you have a problem, or something or someone is
getting you down, where do you go first?

To a friend? A spouse? A confidant?

How often do you mull over something internally until you

are exhausted or it affects you mentally and physically?

We do this all the time.

How often do you bring your problems and worries to God?

Not quite as often, right?

This psalm reminds us that we can and should turn to God when we need someone to talk to—

and when we do, God will hear us.

You know that moment when you think you hear something, and then you tilt your head or turn it towards the sound so you can hear it better?

That's what this psalmist says God does for us when we speak.

"God has turned his ear to me."

Isn't that a beautiful image to have of God?

Turning his ear toward us to better hear what we have to say?

So say it.

Don't hold back.

Are you stressed about something?

Is there something in your life that is bringing you grief or anxiety?

Tell God all about it.

Vent, cry, yell, hurt, ask for help.

Bring all of it to God.

Because God has **promised** to hear us.

God hears our prayers, our fears, our anger, our joys, our sadness, and our anxiety.

God hears it all, and God can handle it all.

There is no grief or anger or stress that is bigger than God.

There is no illness, anxiety, or fear that God can't take.

Trust that when you talk to God, you are heard.

God is listening, so speak.

No flowery language or right words needed.

Just be you. Be honest.

And God will hear you, and be with you.

"And if we know that he hears us—whatever we ask—we know that we have what we asked of him." (1 John 5:15)

Trusting

Trust in the Lord with all your heart, and
lean not on your own understanding.

In all your ways acknowledge Him, and He
shall direct your paths.

PROVERBS 3:5-6

THIS VERSE IS ON my office wall.

It's the first thing I see when I open my door each workday.

That's not by accident.

I believe this is one of the simplest and most difficult things
we are called to do as followers of Christ.

And for me, it's something I need to be reminded of daily.

Trust in God.

But this verse doesn't just say trust in God. It says trust in
God and not in myself.

"Lean not on your own understanding."

The Message paraphrases this verse as, "Don't try to figure everything out on your own."[7]

Oh man.

That's so hard.

Trust in God, not in yourself.

I like to put my trust in a lot of other things besides God: friends, family, doctors, nurses, teachers, preachers, my own health, technology, money, stuff.

And they will all fail.

Even I will fail.

I like to think if I just try hard enough, I can figure it out.

I've got this.

I don't need help.

I want to believe I have all the answers, that I can do it myself, that the way I see the world is the right way.

But it's not.

God calls us to put our trust in God first.

So what does that look like, exactly?

"In all your ways acknowledge him."

Here's where knowing a little Hebrew gets fun.

The word "ways" can also be translated as paths, journey, or course of life.

---

7 Peterson, Eugene. *The Message: The Bible in Contemporary Language*. Colorado Springs, CO: NavPress, 2003, p1091

The word "acknowledge" can also be translated as perceive, find, recognize, or discern.

That changes this verse so much for me:

In all your paths find God.

Recognize God on your course of life.

Discern God as you journey.

We already know God is with us, that he doesn't leave us.

But sometimes we're like those horses with blinders.

We are so stuck looking one way—our way—that we forget to look for God.

We forget to trust God.

God is there, we just miss him.

Lastly, this verse ends with a promise: "God shall direct your paths."

Again, the Hebrew here makes this promise even more significant, because "direct" can also be translated as make smooth, or straighten, or lead.

When we put our trust in God, when we stop relying on things that inevitably fail us or let us down, God makes whatever journey we are on straight.

When we decide to do the impossible, to take off the blinders of the way we think things should be, God is there, leading us with love.

It doesn't mean all the bumps in the road go away, but it does mean God is helping us navigate them.

And God is bigger than any bump or curve or detour our paths might take us on.

So try it.

Put this verse where you need to see it.

Let it be a daily reminder to look for God in your world and trust that God is with you, loving you, and leading you on your way.

Unafraid

Do not fear, for I am with you, do not be
afraid for I am your God;
I will strengthen you, I will help you, I will
uphold you with my victorious right hand.

ISAIAH 41:10

THERE ARE SO MANY things to be afraid of, and the list is
always growing.

Guns.

Aging.

Cancer.

Terrorism.

Car accidents.

The unknown.

These are just the start of a very long list.

On the day Jesus died, things seemed pretty hopeless.

It was a day where it looked like evil won.

And for the disciples of Jesus, seeing him on that cross was the definition of hopelessness.

They could not believe what they were seeing.

They could not fathom that this was where their journey as Christ's followers ended.

And they were scared.

They were afraid they'd be killed as well.

They were afraid that they had missed something, that maybe they had followed the wrong guy.

We feel this way too sometimes when life gets scary.

When it seems like fear is winning the day.

This scripture from Isaiah is one of the many times in the Bible that we hear the phrases "do not fear" and "do not be afraid."

Isaiah knew that on dark days, we need the reminder that God's got us.

When we think we've lost the battle, we need the reminder of who will win the war.

God's got this.

God's got you.

Giving you strength, giving you help, holding you up when you cannot do it yourself.

God's got you.

There is a saying you may have heard: The Bible says "do not fear" 365 times. That's enough for every day of the year.

I don't know if it's true or not. I haven't actually gone through the Bible and counted all the times someone says to not be afraid, but I don't think the actual number is the point.

We **need** a daily reminder to not be afraid.

So start with this reminder from Isaiah.

Memorize it. Say it out loud to start your day.

Print it out and look at it as often as you feel afraid.

And remember that no matter what it is that we fear, God is bigger.

That no matter how large and overwhelming our fear feels, God's love is larger.

Let's be honest: sometimes our fear feels pretty huge.

Sometimes it feels like the only option.

Sometimes it feels like it's won the day.

But unlike the disciples, we know how the story ends.

We know that just days after he was on that cross, Jesus rose.

The tomb is empty.

Love ultimately conquers death.

Fear may have us today, but love gets the last word, the final say.

Love wins.

Love always, always, wins.

Peace

Peace I leave with you, my peace I give to you. I do not give to you as the world gives.

Do not let your hearts be troubled, and do not let them be afraid.

JOHN 14:27

"PEACE BE WITH YOU."

You've heard it before.

Maybe at church.

Maybe to begin or end a prayer or conversation.

Peace.

We don't always realize that this phrase is given to us by Jesus.

Not some ancient Christian person, not a theologian or pope, but Jesus.

And Jesus said these words of peace at pretty key times in his ministry.

When Jesus was predicting his death to the disciples, he reminded them, "Peace I leave with you."

When the disciples were in hiding, huddled in a locked room because they were afraid of what might happen next, Jesus came into the room and said, "My peace be with you."

And again, when a risen Jesus met some disciples on the road, he said, "My peace be with you."

The key word in each of these instances is "my."

Peace is a gift from God.

Jesus tells his disciples that he doesn't work like the world works.

What he gives is different from what the world gives.

Peace is not found in all those places we try to look for it.

It's not found in relationships.

It's not found in possessions.

It's not found in our health or wellbeing.

Peace is found through and with God.

It's a gift.

Already given.

Does your life seem peaceful today?

Does it feel calm and quiet and restful?

Or does it feel chaotic and panicked and fearful?

"Do not let your hearts be troubled."

When the disciples are the most fearful, the most troubled, the most anxious,

Jesus appears and gives them peace.

As if they just needed a reminder.

"Hey guys, remember me? You've got this."

The more I think about this, the more I think that trust and peace go hand in hand.

Because God has already shown up.

God has already said those words to us.

Peace be with you.

You.

Not just that other guy over there, but you.

And not because of something you did or didn't do,

but simply because God is a God of peace, and you are a chosen and beloved child of God.

That's it.

The disciples needed the reminder of God's peace in their most anxious moments.

And so do we.

So here it is.

Jesus is reminding us today to trust.

Trust that God has already given us the peace we so desperately need.

"Hey guys, remember me? You've got this."

So do it.

Give yourself a break.

The God of all peace will meet you where you are.

"Now may the Lord of peace himself give you peace at all times in all ways. The Lord be with all of you."

(2 Thessalonians 3:16)

Crazy Busy

"Martha, Martha," the Lord answered, "You are worried and upset about many things, but few things are needed—or indeed only one.

Mary has chosen what is better, and it will not be taken from her."

LUKE 10:41-42

JESUS CAME TO VISIT Martha at her home. Martha was unhappy that her sister Mary was just sitting around listening to Jesus while she was working hard to make sure everything was perfect.

Tell her to help me, Jesus! Don't you see how busy I am?

And Jesus responds with our verses for today. "You are worried and upset about many things."

Oh, Martha. She was so frantic about getting things ready for Jesus, she forgot all *about* Jesus!

I'd like to think I'm Mary in this story, sitting quietly and calmly at the feet of Jesus, but I know I'm Martha.

And let's be real—most of us are more Martha than Mary.

We are busy.

Crazy busy.

And that's not bad. In fact, Jesus doesn't tell Martha what she is doing is wrong.

I mean, they are going to need to eat, and need places to sit, so the things she does aren't unnecessary.

She only wanted some help from her sister.

She wasn't thinking what Mary was doing was important or valuable.

How often do we do that?

How often do we assume that what we are doing is the most important thing?

That there can't possibly be something that is higher up on the list than our stuff?

Oh, Martha.

There is something better.

Your stuff isn't bad, but there is something better than running around, worrying, and being stressed out.

Really.

And it's Jesus.

So today, in the middle of your to-do lists, your stress and worry and running around, take some time to sit with Jesus.

Take out your Bible.

Find this whole story, Luke 10:38–42.

Hear what Jesus is saying to you today:

Being with me is the one thing.

It's the only thing you need.

I am the better thing.

Or find another section of your Bible to read. It doesn't matter which one. Just come sit with Jesus.

In the midst of your busy day, I promise it's okay to sit in stillness for a bit.

Your stuff will still be there when you get back.

But this is better.

PS: This week, be an uplifter by giving someone in your life the gift of time. Run an errand for them. Cook a meal. Watch their kids so they can have just a few minutes of stillness. Give them something better than busy.

Strength in numbers

Have I not commanded you?
Be strong and courageous.

Do not be terrified; do not be
discouraged, for the Lord your God will
be with you wherever you go.

JOSHUA 1:9

THIS MAY BE A FAMILIAR VERSE.

Maybe you learned it in Sunday school, or at camp, or
maybe when you went on a trip. It's a reminder that God
goes with us.

And it's never bad to remember God goes with us when we
travel.

It's not horrible to be reminded that God isn't just in a
church building on Sunday mornings.

But if you consider this little section in its broader context,
it's a bit bigger.

At the start of the book of Joshua, Moses has just died, and we find God calling Joshua to step into the role vacated by Moses to lead the people of Israel.

Can you imagine what Joshua was feeling at that moment?

His friend and mentor has just died and he's expected to step into his shoes and keep going?

It's heart-wrenching and terrifying at the same time.

Not only is Joshua dealing with his grief, which is hard enough on its own, he's also now dealing with this mantle of responsibility that has been placed on his shoulders.

It's a lot.

It's maybe even too much.

Have you ever felt like Joshua?

Have you ever felt like just saying,

"It's too much, God.

You're asking too much.

I can't do anything more."

In Joshua 1:5, God makes a promise to Joshua that day:

"As I was with Moses, so I will be with you.

I will never leave you or forsake you."

Believe it or not, in our baptism, *we* were given this same promise.

God is with us.

God will never leave us.

Does that mean, like Joshua, we won't grieve the loss of someone we love?

Does that mean we won't wonder how we can do what God is calling us to do?

No.

What it does mean is that we're not alone.

We don't grieve alone.

We don't struggle alone.

We don't do anything alone.

God is always with us.

Whatever happens. Wherever we go.

It's a promise that I hope you hear today.

So be strong and courageous.

And go with God.

You are not alone.

Acknowledgments

The creation of this book grew out of a community of people who loved me and encouraged me to dream bigger than I would have on my own:

To the Cancer Support Group at Prince of Peace, for being the group of people that I write to and for and with. You inspire me daily and I am so honored that you let me be a part of your lives and journey.

To Dara at WiseInk, for being the biggest "dream bigger!!!" champion of them all. You made a glimmer of an idea into a reality and I feel lucky to work with you and your entire team.

To Emily and Scott, designer people extraordinaires, who have gifts I can't even dream of having and managed to create exactly what was in my brain all along. Uplift looks amazing because of you both!

To Megan, for being the cheerleader of all cheerleaders, who listened and dreamed with me long into the night, who supported me even when I wasn't sure what the next step was, and who never let me stay on the ground level for very long. Two tickets to the first UC are all yours.

To the Book Club. Though that title doesn't even come close to encompassing what you all are to me, thanks for the happy hours, the conversation, the prayers, the retreats, the vacations, and most of all - thanks for seeing me as something more beautiful and amazing than I ever saw myself. You make me feel like the masterpiece I am.

To my family, who have never once been surprised by the

things that happen in my life. You just say "of course" - like my dreams were always the outcome you expected. Your faith in me and my ability to accomplish big things has been unwavering and I am so thankful you're my people.

To Layla, you make my life funnier, louder, messier, sweeter, and more beautiful than I ever could have imagined. You are my uplift every day. Thanks for always dancing with me, for always telling me "you've got this Mom," and for the daily snuggles. I couldn't do this without you.

To Sam, for quietly and calmly supporting me no matter how not quiet and not calm I was in return. Nothing seems impossible when you're with me. You are the love of my life.

TeamTerfa FTW.

About Natalia Terfa

NATÁLIA TERFA is a pastor at Prince of Peace Lutheran Church in Brooklyn Park, Minnesota.

She is passionate about grace, yoga, and books. Natalia lives with her husband, daughter, and fluffy cat in Minneapolis, Minnesota, where she daily strives to combine her passions and her people into one awesome life.

You can contact Natalia for questions, comments or speaking: natalia@upliftlife.org

Or follow her on Facebook, Twitter, and Instagram.

Connect with the Uplift Community and be a part of #TeamUplift at UpliftLife.org, Facebook (@UpliftLifeCommunity), Twitter (@Uplift_Life), and Instagram (@UpliftCommunity).